Ready·Set·Learn......

Printing Practice

Grades K–1

180+ Stickers Inside

Managing Editor
Ina Massler Levin, M.A.

Editor
Eric Migliaccio

Contributing Editor
Sarah Smith

Creative Director
Karen J. Goldfluss, M.S. Ed.

Cover Design
Tony Carrillo / Marilyn Goldberg

Teacher Created Resources, Inc.
6421 Industry Way
Westminster, CA 92683
www.teachercreated.com

ISBN: 978-1-4206-5967-2

©2007 Teacher Created Resources, Inc.
Reprinted, 2013 (PO6107)

Made in U.S.A.

Teacher Created Resources

This book belongs to

_____

Ready·Set·Learn

Get Ready to Learn!

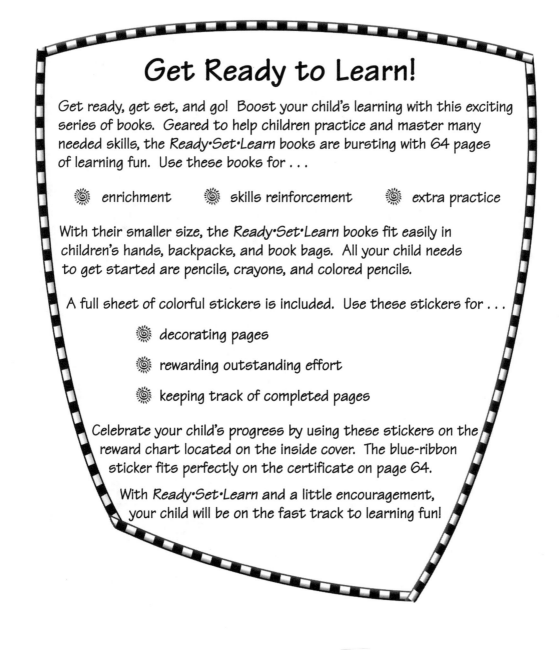

Get ready, get set, and go! Boost your child's learning with this exciting series of books. Geared to help children practice and master many needed skills, the *Ready·Set·Learn* books are bursting with 64 pages of learning fun. Use these books for . . .

- enrichment
- skills reinforcement
- extra practice

With their smaller size, the *Ready·Set·Learn* books fit easily in children's hands, backpacks, and book bags. All your child needs to get started are pencils, crayons, and colored pencils.

A full sheet of colorful stickers is included. Use these stickers for . . .

- decorating pages
- rewarding outstanding effort
- keeping track of completed pages

Celebrate your child's progress by using these stickers on the reward chart located on the inside cover. The blue-ribbon sticker fits perfectly on the certificate on page 64.

With *Ready·Set·Learn* and a little encouragement, your child will be on the fast track to learning fun!

The Alphabet

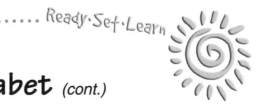

The Alphabet *(cont.)*

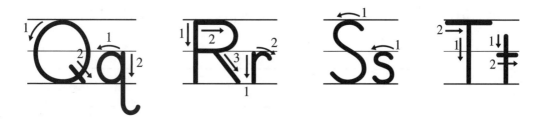

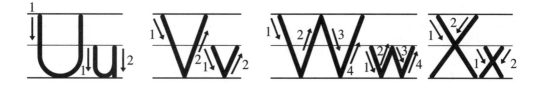

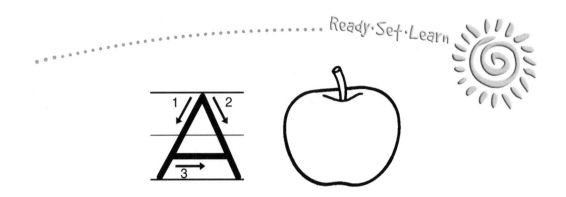

Directions: Trace each letter and word. Then write them as many times as you can.

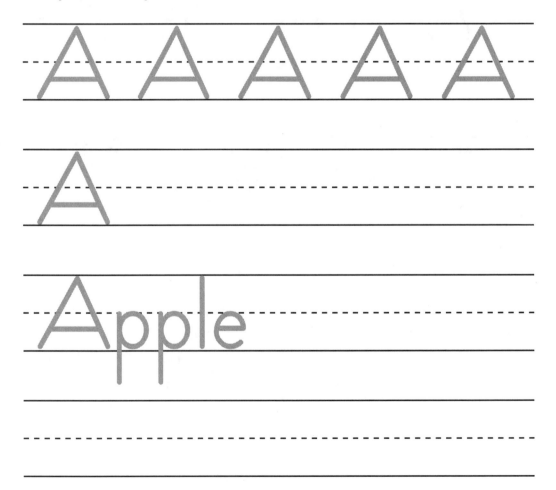

Directions: Trace each letter and word. Then write them as many times as you can.

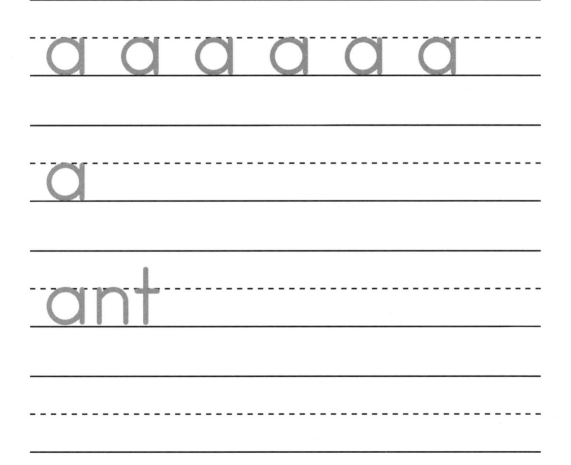

Ready·Set·Learn

Directions: Trace each letter and word. Then write them as many times as you can.

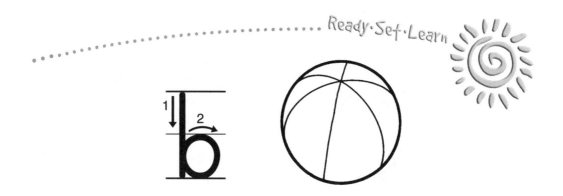

Directions: Trace each letter and word. Then write them as many times as you can.

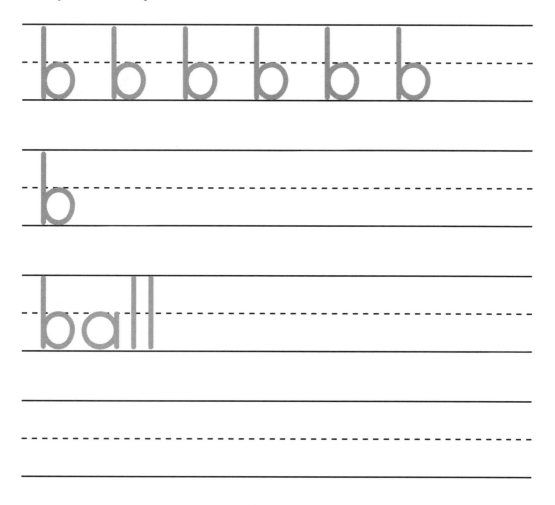

Directions: Trace each letter and word. Then write them as many times as you can.

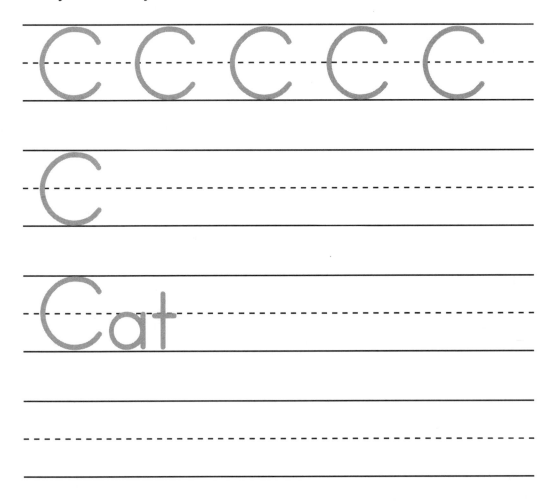

C

1

Directions: Trace each letter and word. Then write them as many times as you can.

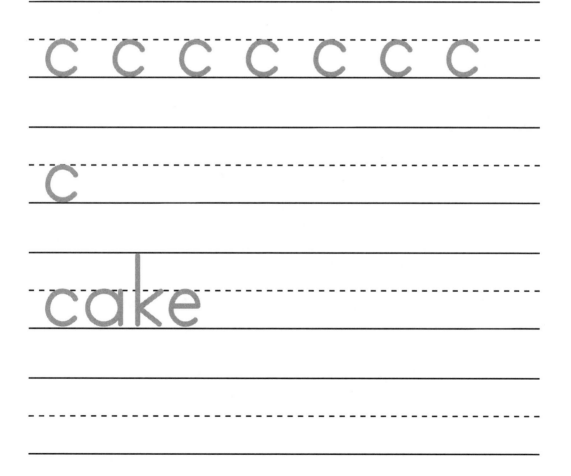

C C C C C C C

c

cake

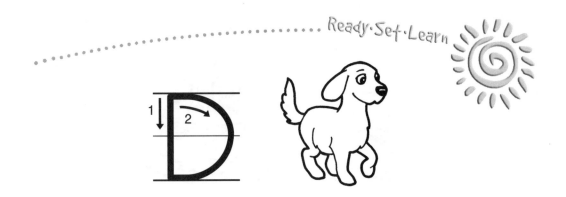

Directions: Trace each letter and word. Then write them as many times as you can.

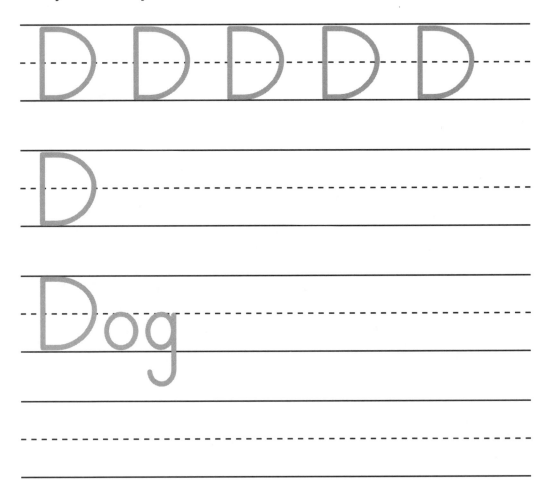

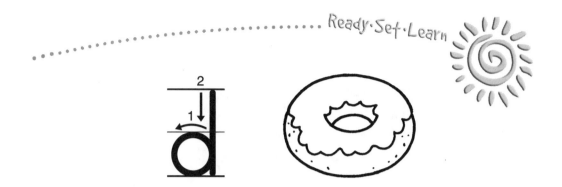

Directions: Trace each letter and word. Then write them as many times as you can.

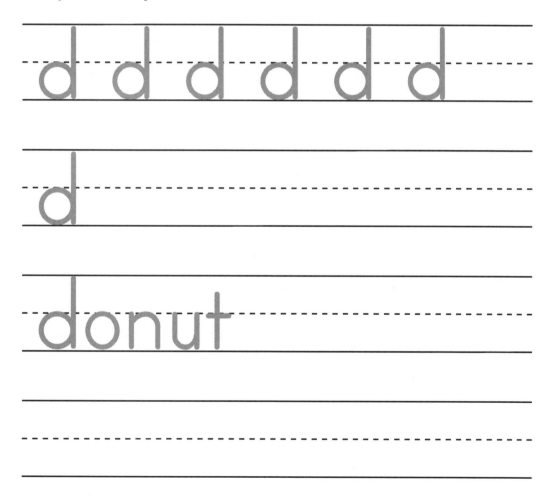

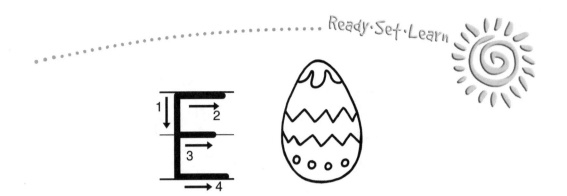

Directions: Trace each letter and word. Then write them as many times as you can.

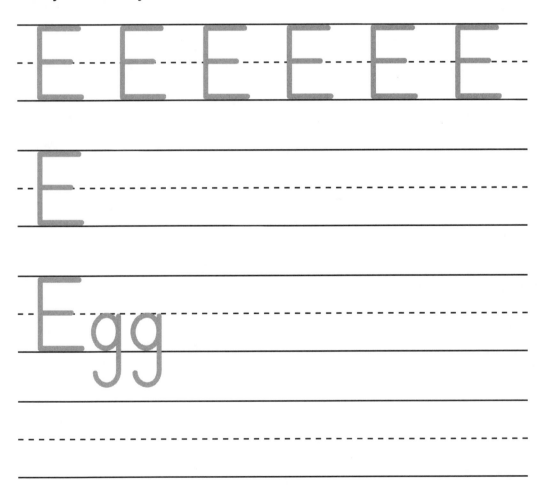

14

Directions: Trace each letter and word. Then write them as many times as you can.

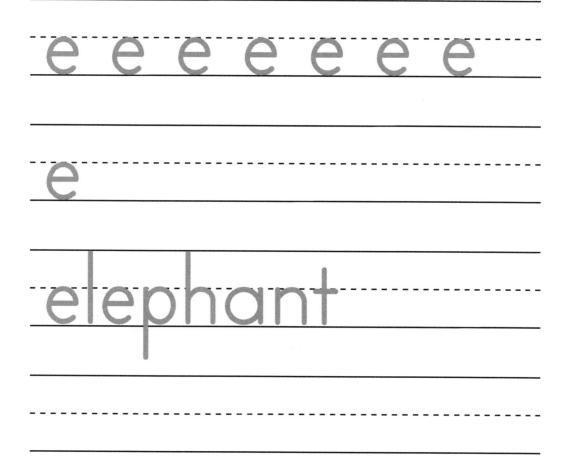

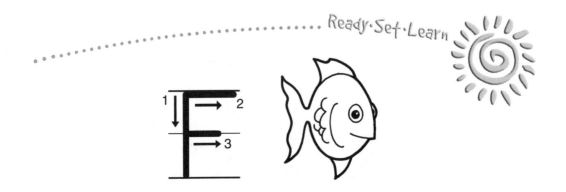

Directions: Trace each letter and word. Then write them as many times as you can.

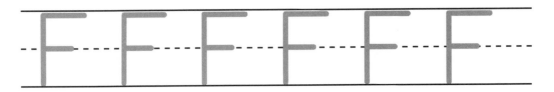

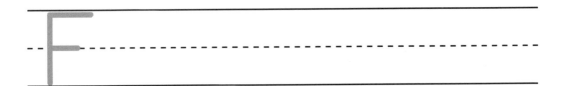

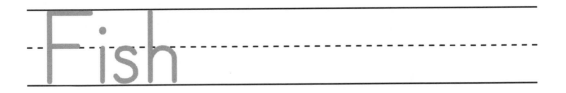

16   ©Teacher Created Resources, Inc.

Directions: Trace each letter and word. Then write them as many times as you can.

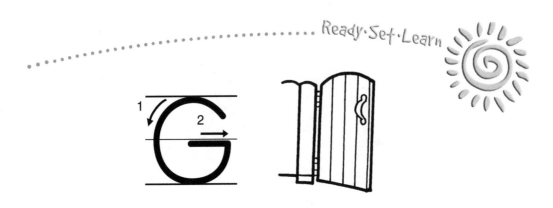

Directions: Trace each letter and word. Then write them as many times as you can.

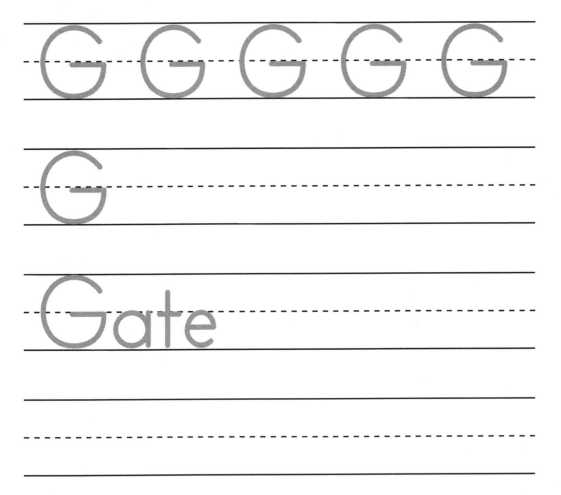

Directions: Trace each letter and word. Then write them as many times as you can.

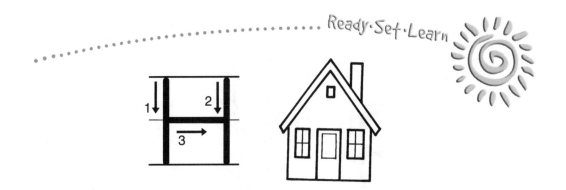

Ready·Set·Learn

Directions: Trace each letter and word. Then write them as many times as you can.

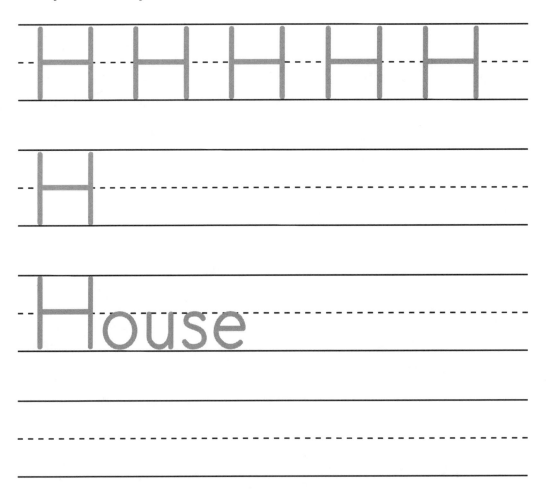

Directions: Trace each letter and word. Then write them as many times as you can.

h h h h h h h

h

hat

Directions: Trace each letter and word. Then write them as many times as you can.

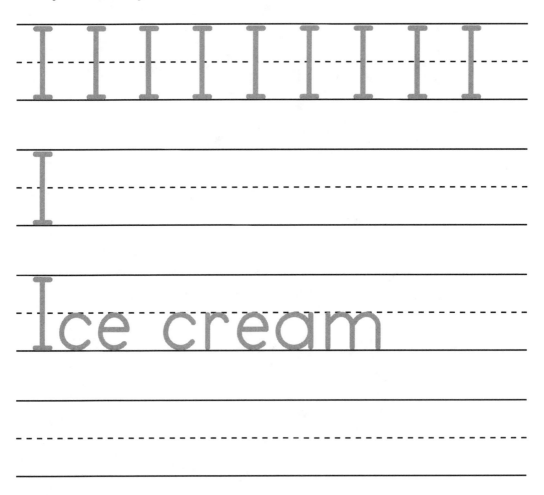

I I I I I I I I I

I

Ice cream

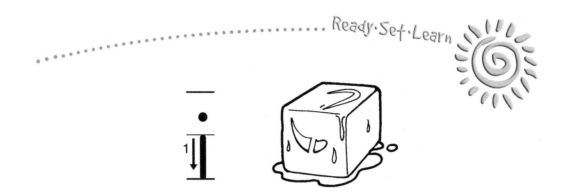

Directions: Trace each letter and word. Then write them as many times as you can.

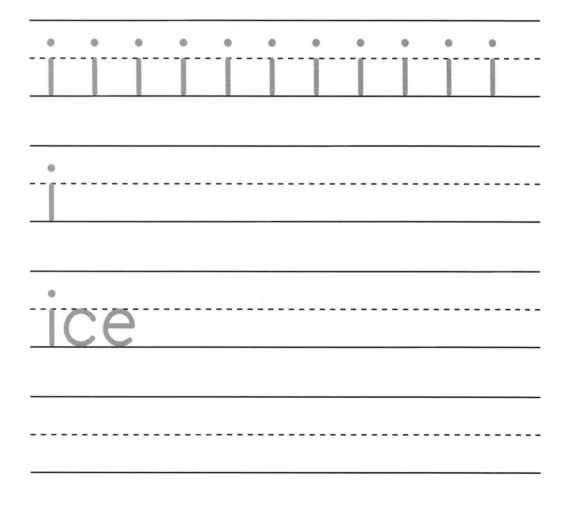

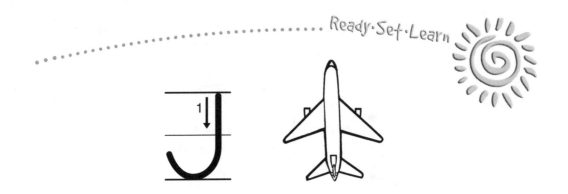

Directions: Trace each letter and word. Then write them as many times as you can.

24

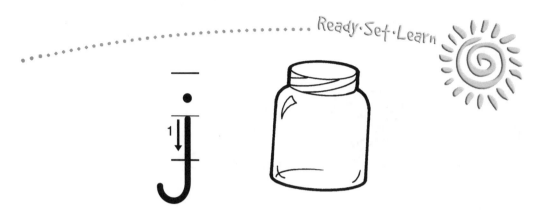

Directions: Trace each letter and word. Then write them as many times as you can.

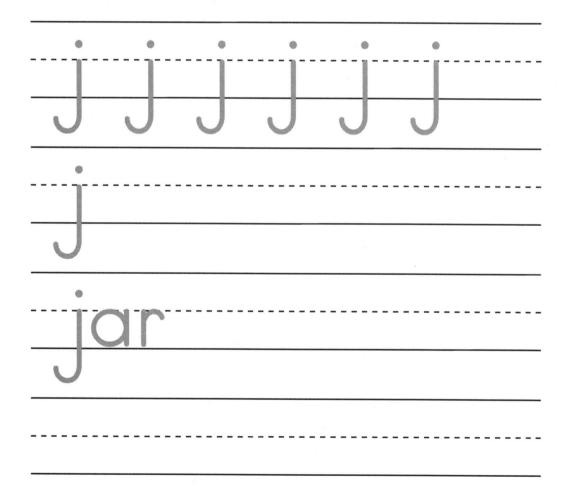

j j j j j j

j

jar

Ready·Set·Learn

Directions: Trace each letter and word. Then write them as many times as you can.

K K K K K

K

Kangaroo

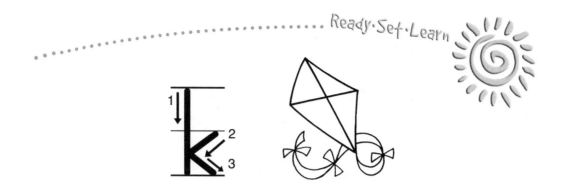

Directions: Trace each letter and word. Then write them as many times as you can.

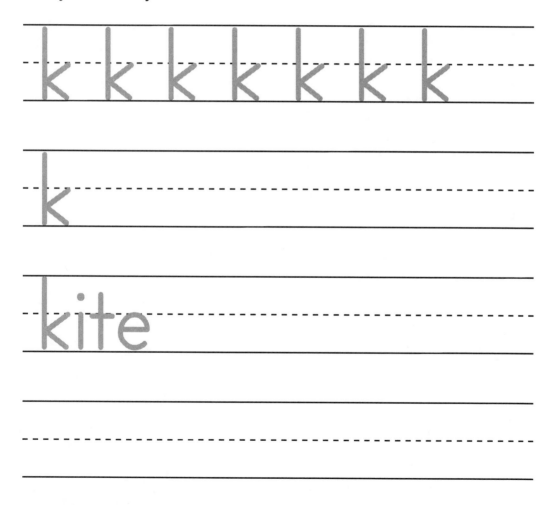

k k k k k k k

k

kite

Directions: Trace each letter and word. Then write them as many times as you can.

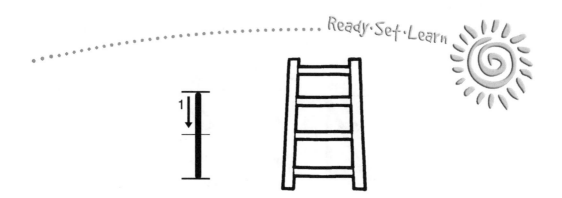

Directions: Trace each letter and word. Then write them as many times as you can.

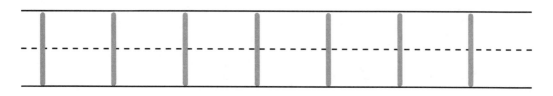

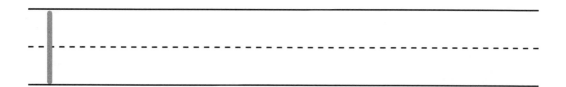

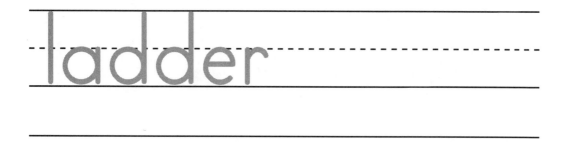

ladder

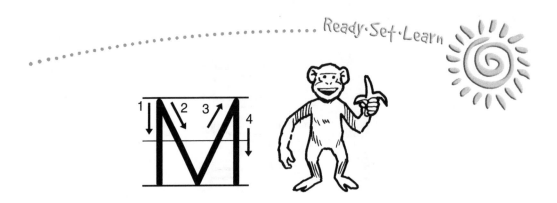

Directions: Trace each letter and word. Then write them as many times as you can.

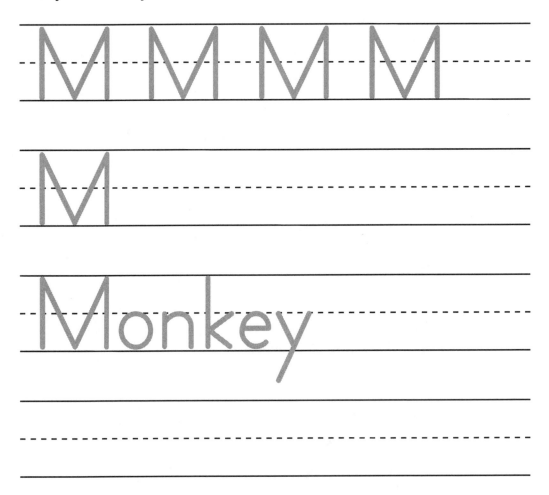

30

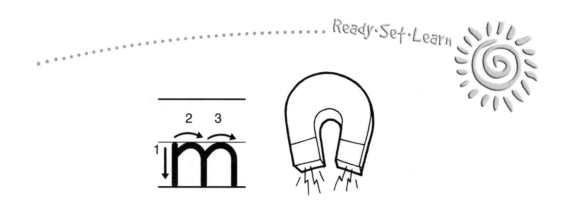

Directions: Trace each letter and word. Then write them as many times as you can.

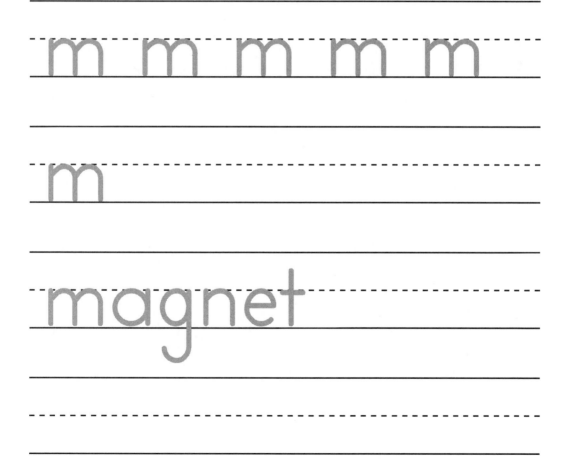

m m m m m

m

magnet

Directions: Trace each letter and word. Then write them as many times as you can.

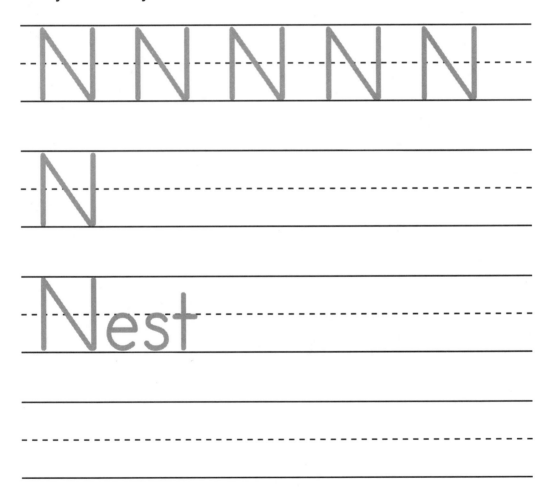

32

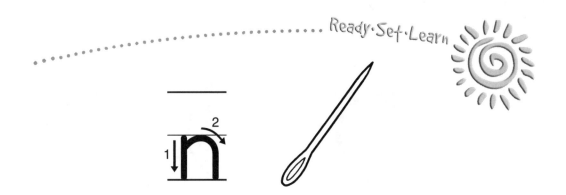

Directions: Trace each letter and word. Then write them as many times as you can.

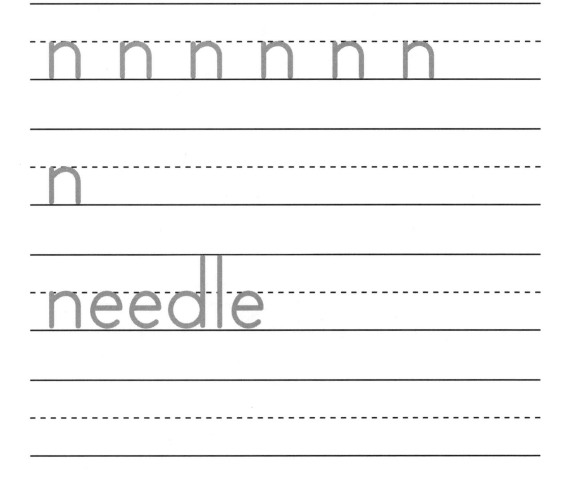

n n n n n n

n

needle

Directions: Trace each letter and word. Then write them as many times as you can.

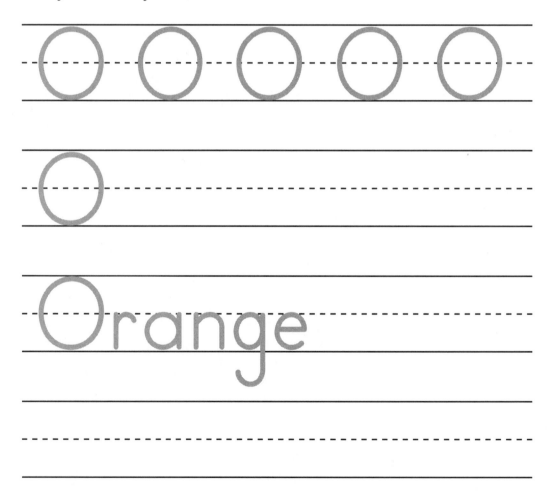

Ready·Set·Learn

Directions: Trace each letter and word. Then write them as many times as you can.

o o o o o o

o

octopus

Directions: Trace each letter and word. Then write them as many times as you can.

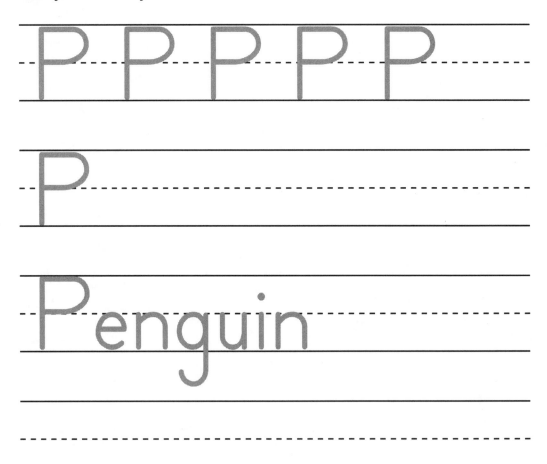

P P P P P

P

Penguin

36

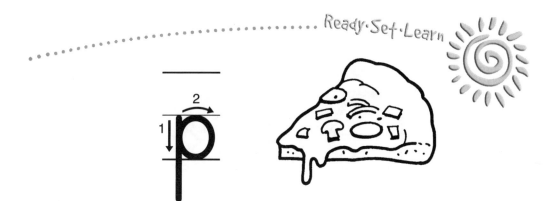

Directions: Trace each letter and word. Then write them as many times as you can.

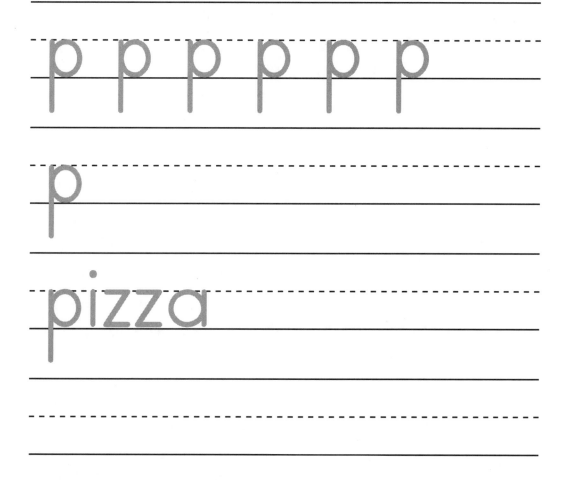

p p p p p p

p

pizza

Directions: Trace each letter and word. Then write them as many times as you can.

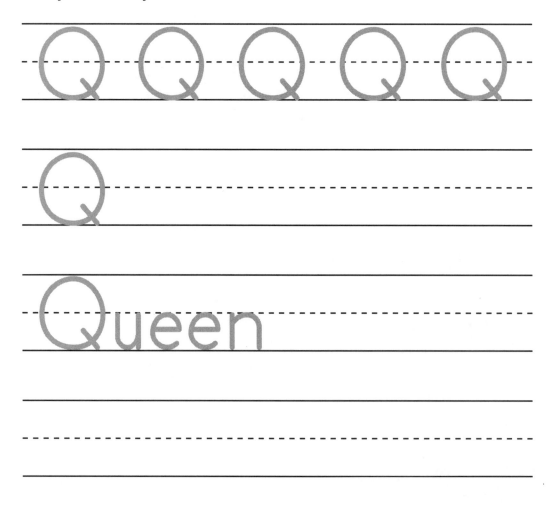

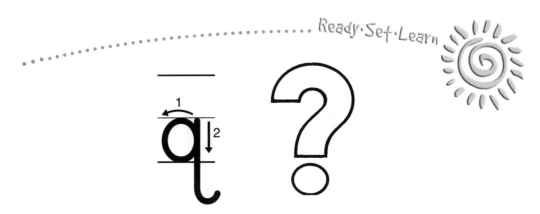

Directions: Trace each letter and word. Then write them as many times as you can.

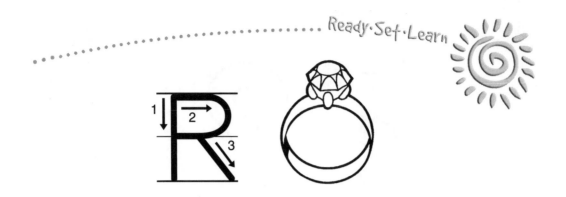

Ready·Set·Learn

Directions: Trace each letter and word. Then write them as many times as you can.

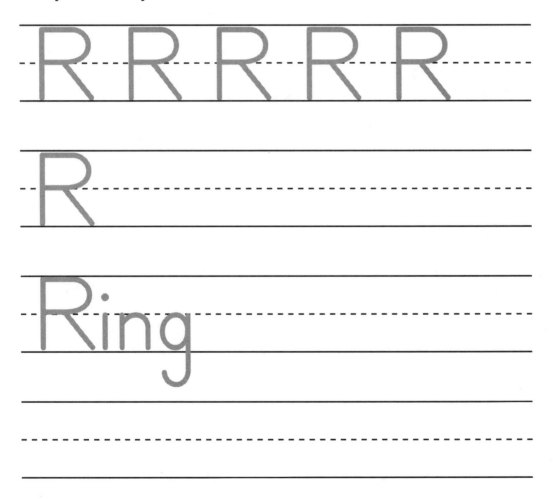

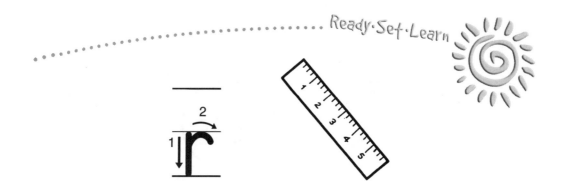

Directions: Trace each letter and word. Then write them as many times as you can.

r r r r r r r

r

ruler

Directions: Trace each letter and word. Then write them as many times as you can.

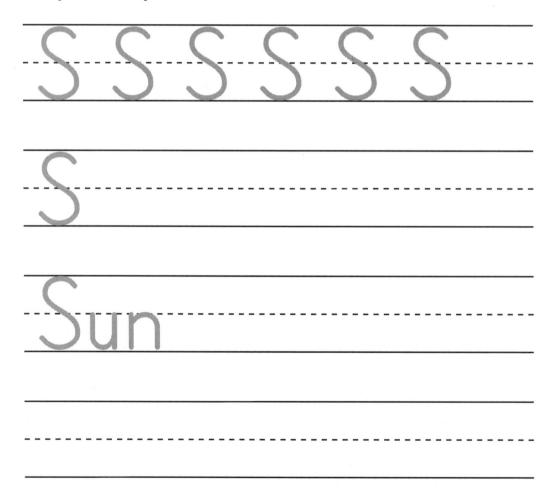

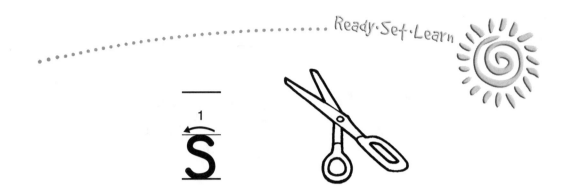

Directions: Trace each letter and word. Then write them as many times as you can.

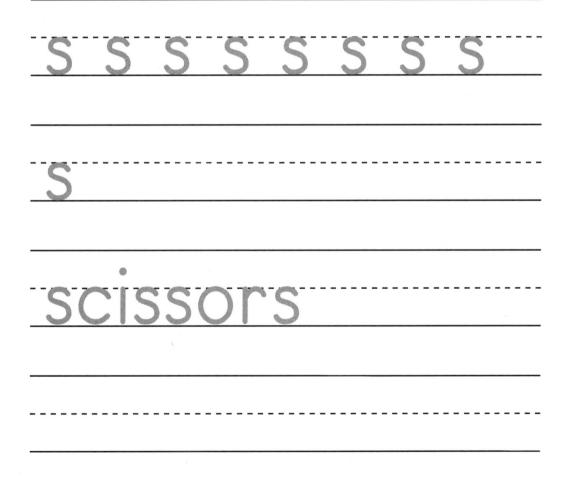

S S S S S S S S

s

scissors

Directions: Trace each letter and word. Then write them as many times as you can.

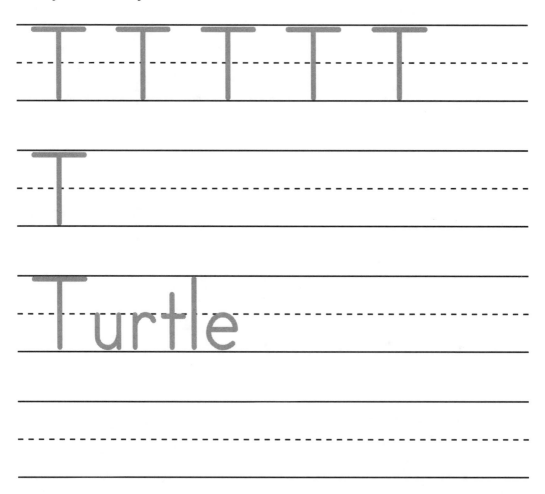

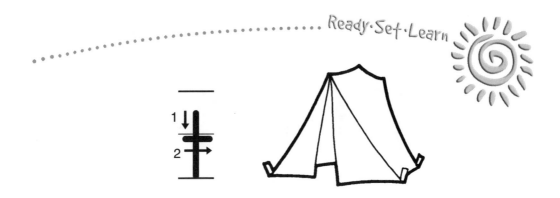

Ready · Set · Learn

Directions: Trace each letter and word. Then write them as many times as you can.

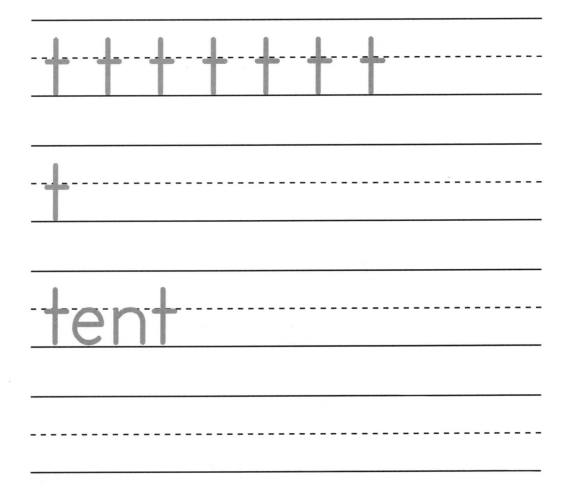

Directions: Trace each letter and word. Then write them as many times as you can.

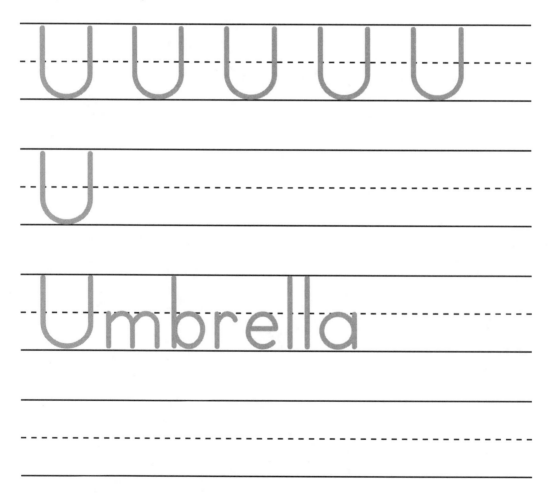

46

Directions: Trace each letter and word. Then write them as many times as you can.

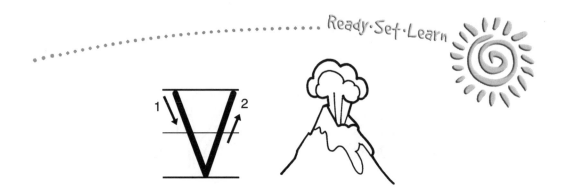

Directions: Trace each letter and word. Then write them as many times as you can.

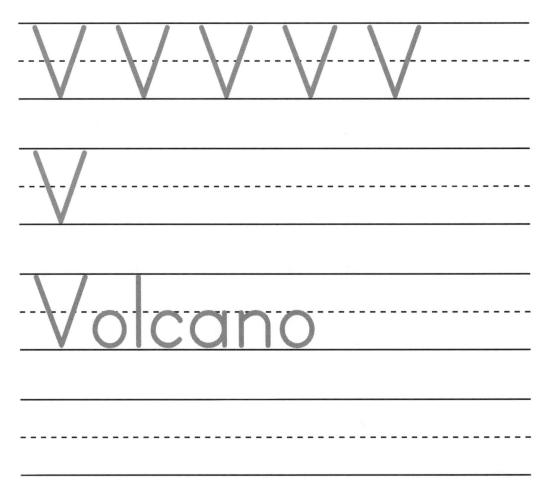

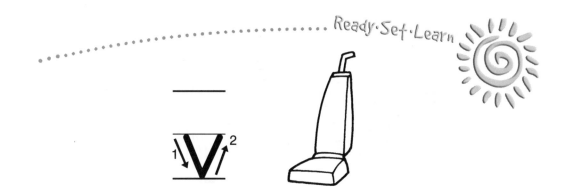

Directions: Trace each letter and word. Then write them as many times as you can.

V V V V V V V

V

vacuum

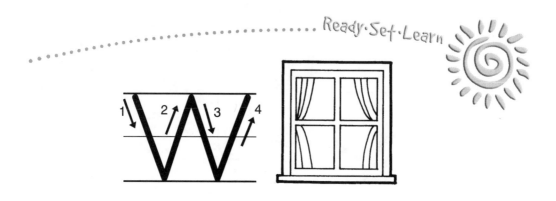

Directions: Trace each letter and word. Then write them as many times as you can.

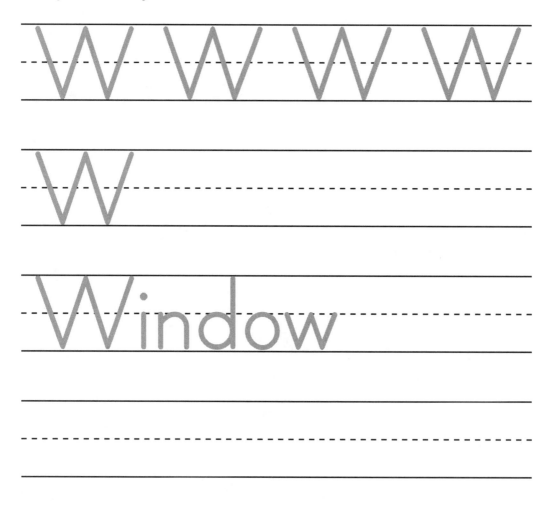

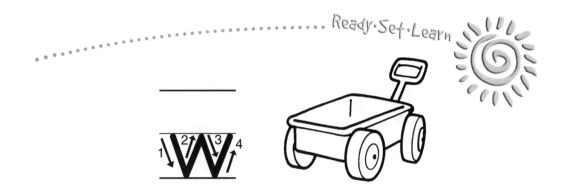

Directions: Trace each letter and word. Then write them as many times as you can.

W W W W W

W

wagon

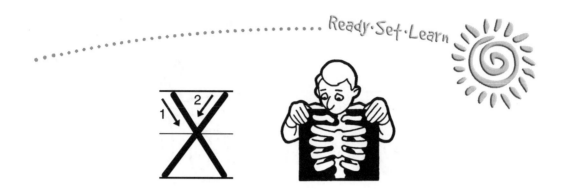

Directions: Trace each letter and word. Then write them as many times as you can.

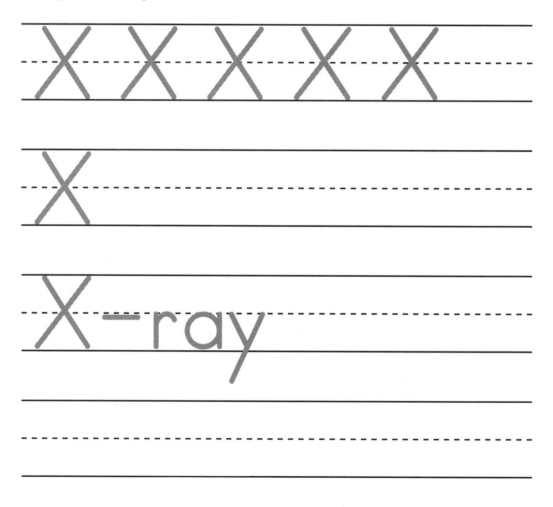

52

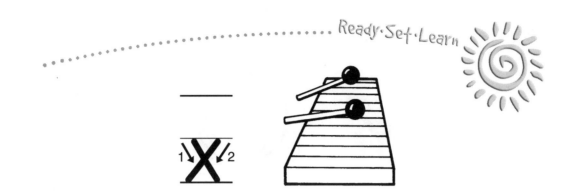

Ready·Set·Learn

Directions: Trace each letter and word. Then write them as many times as you can.

X X X X X X X

x

xylophone

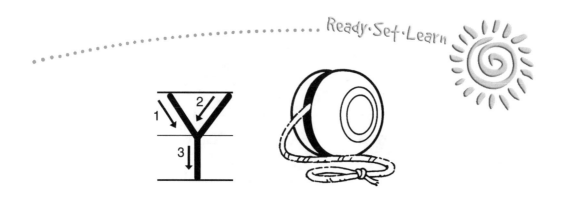

Directions: Trace each letter and word. Then write them as many times as you can.

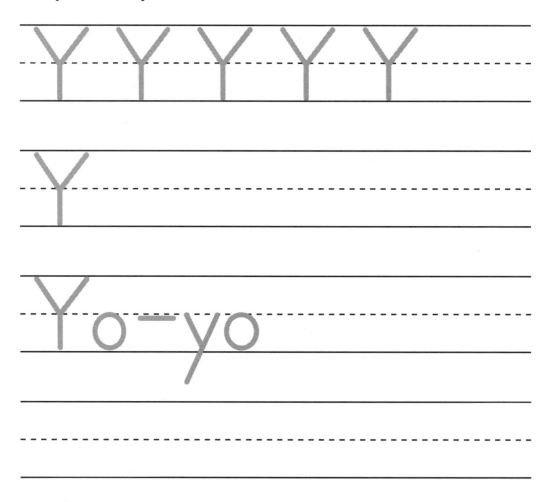

Y o-yo

54

Ready·Set·Learn

Directions: Trace each letter and word. Then write them as many times as you can.

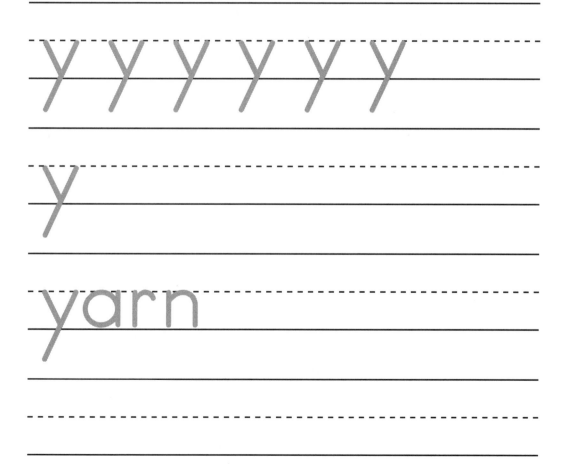

y y y y y y

y

yarn

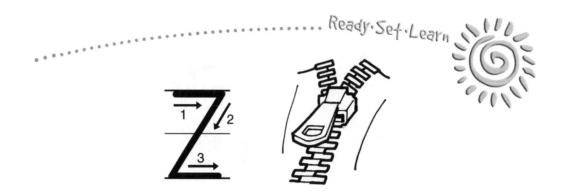

Directions: Trace each letter and word. Then write them as many times as you can.

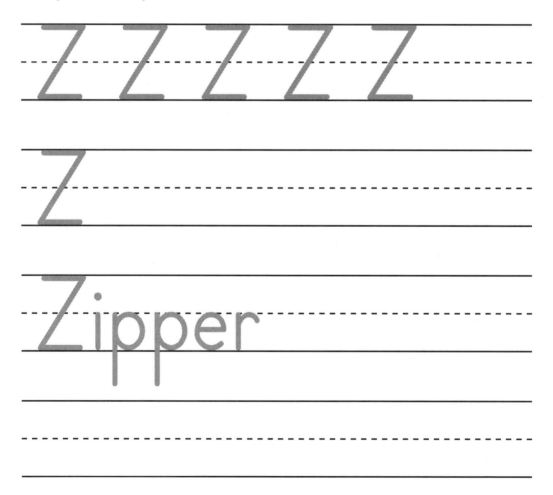

Z Z Z Z Z

Z

Zipper

56

Directions: Trace each letter and word. Then write them as many times as you can.

z z z z z z z

z

zebra

Letter Combinations

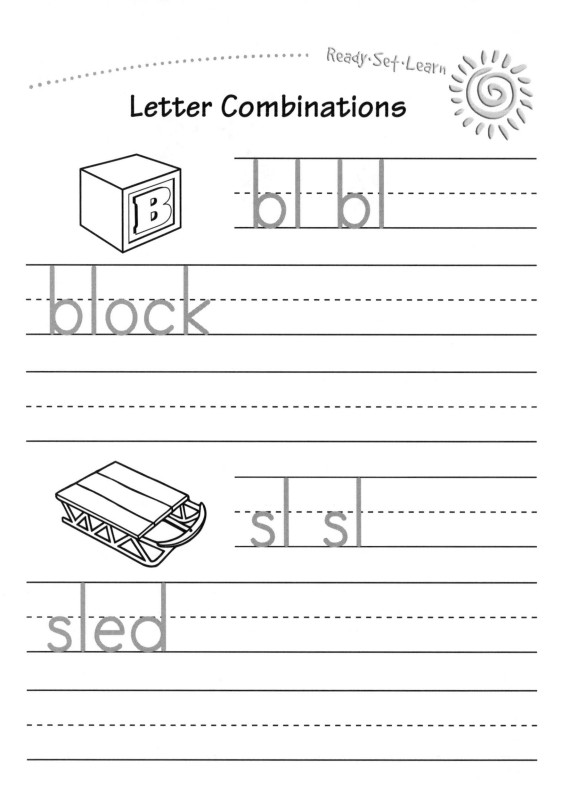

b| b|

block

s| s|

sled

Letter Combinations

fr fr

frog

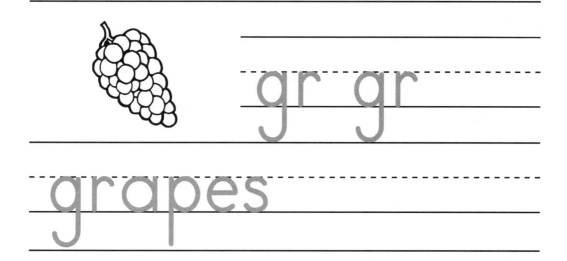
gr gr

grapes

Ready·Set·Learn

Letter Combinations

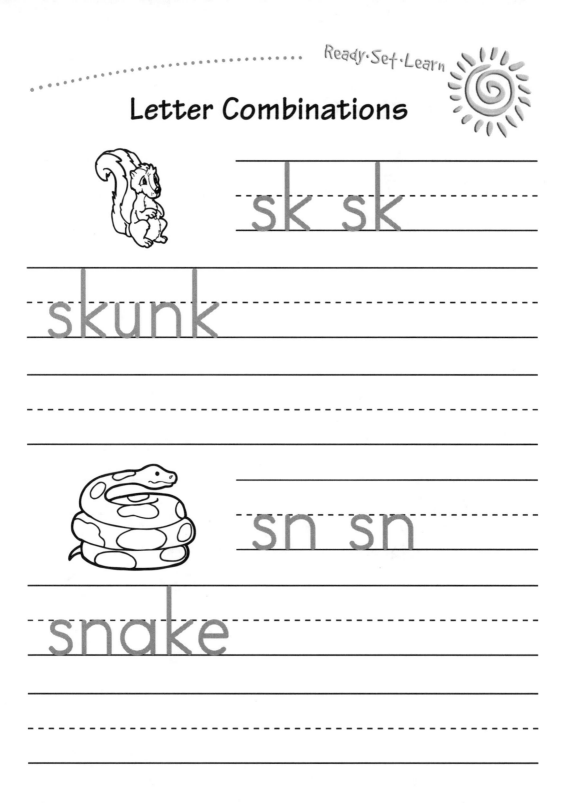

sk sk

skunk

sn sn

snake

Letter Combinations

ai ai

pail

ay ay

hay

Letter Combinations

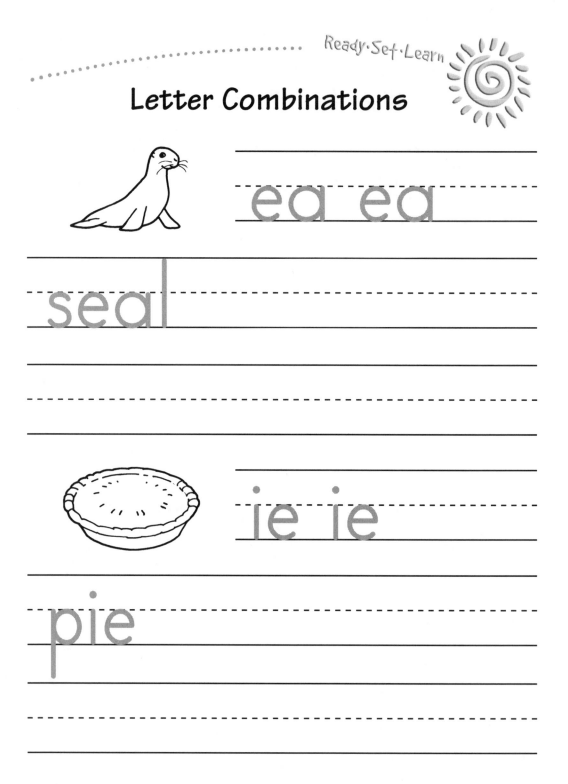

ea ea

seal

ie ie

pie

62

This Award
Is Presented To

_____

for

★ Doing Your Best

★ Trying Hard

★ Not Giving Up

★ Making a
   Great Effort